Wonders of America

Mount Rushmore

For Brannon, of course!—M. D. B.

To Lisa and Benjamin—J. G. W.

ALADDIN PAPERBACKS
An imprint of Simon & Schuster Children's Publishing Division
1230 Avenue of the Americas, New York, NY 10020

Designed by Christopher Grassi
The text of this book was set in Century Oldstyle.
Manufactured in the United States of America
First Aladdin Paperbacks edition May 2007
8 10 9
Library of Congress Cataloging-in-Publication Data
Bauer, Marion Dane.
Mount Rushmore / by Marion Dane Bauer ; illustrated by John Wallace.
1st Aladdin Paperbacks ed.
p. cm.—(Wonders of America)
ISBN-13: 978-1-4169-3477-6 (pbk.)
ISBN-10: 1-4169-3477-4 (pbk.)
ISBN-13: 978-1-4169-3478-3 (lib. ed.)
ISBN-10: 1-4169-3478-2 (lib. ed.)
1. Mount Rushmore National Memorial (S.D.)—Juvenile literature.
I. Wallace, John, 1966– ill. II. Title.
F657.R8B385 2007
978.3'93—dc22
2006029285
0214 LAK

Wonders of America

Mount Rushmore

By Marion Dane Bauer

Illustrated by John Wallace

Ready-to-Read
ALADDIN
New York London Toronto Sydney

The four famous faces
on Mount Rushmore
began with one man's dream.

Doane Robinson dreamed
of a sculptor who
could carve a mountain.

He dreamed of explorers
like Lewis and Clark

or Indian leaders
like Chief Red Cloud
carved into the rock
of the Black Hills.

He found the man
for the job,
Gutzon Borglum.

When Borglum saw
the beautiful Black Hills,
he called them
a “garden of the gods.”

When he saw Mount Rushmore,
he said, "American history
shall march along
that skyline."

He decided to carve
four American presidents.

George Washington,
because Washington was
our first president and the
father of our country.

Thomas Jefferson,
because Jefferson had a vision
of a country reaching from
coast to coast.

Abraham Lincoln,
because Lincoln held the
United States together during
a time of civil war.

Theodore Roosevelt,
because Roosevelt
led our country
to become a great power.

From 1927 to 1941 Borglum and nearly 400 workers worked in sun, wind . . .

. . . and bone-chilling cold
to carve the mountain.

The monument is very big.
Each head is sixty feet tall.

Roosevelt's moustache
is twenty feet across.

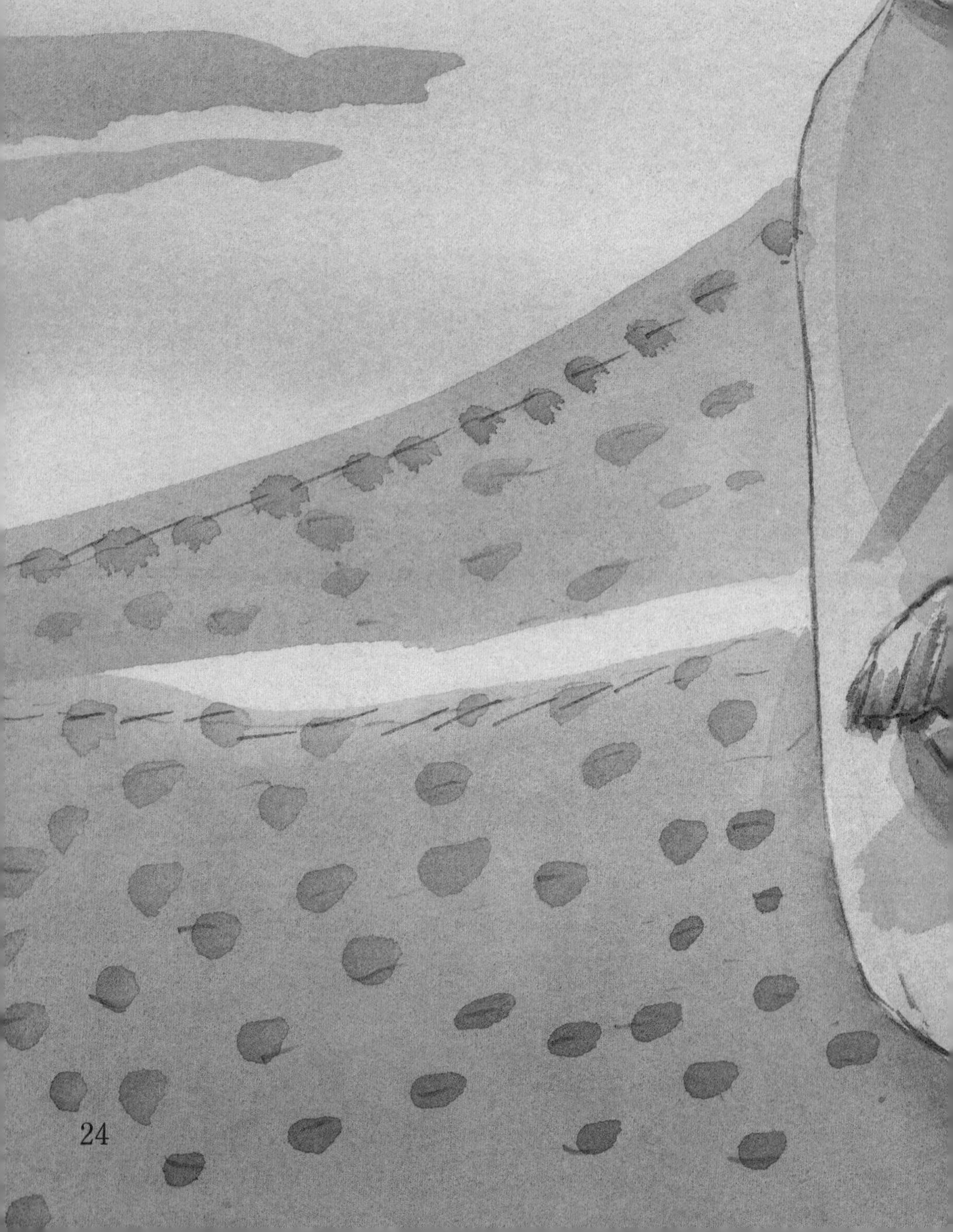

Washington's nose
is twenty feet long.
Each eye is
eleven feet wide.

Millions of people
visit Mount Rushmore
every year.

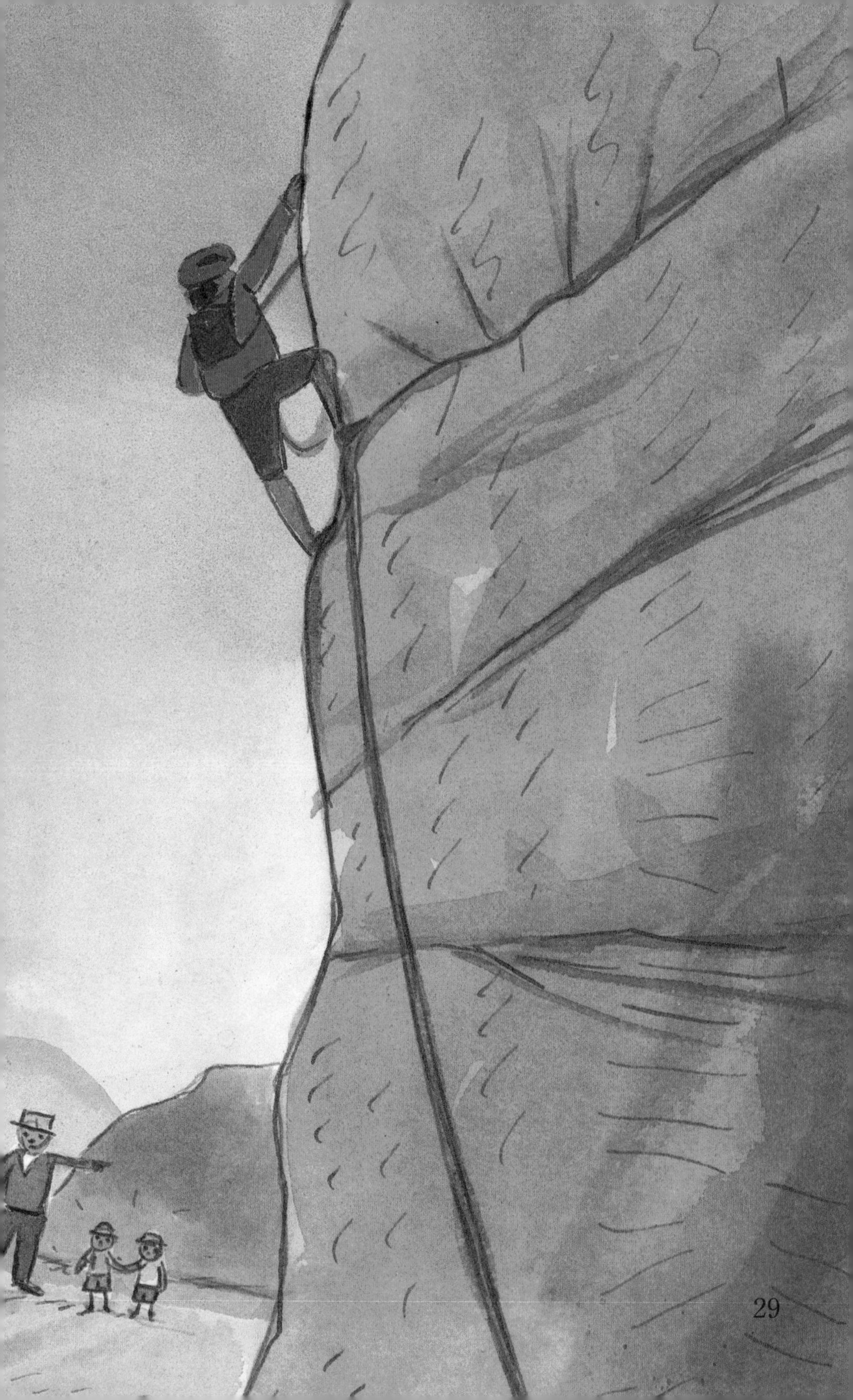

Borglum wanted
Mount Rushmore to be
a shrine of democracy.
And it is.

Interesting Facts about Mount Rushmore

★ Nearly 500,000 tons of stone were blasted from Mount Rushmore to carve the four heads.

★ Borglum removed 20 feet of surface rock before he found rock solid enough to carve Washington. Jefferson and Lincoln are some 60 feet inside Mount Rushmore. Roosevelt is between 100 and 120 feet in.

★ The Mount Rushmore granite is extremely hard. It is among the oldest rock in the world. Geologists say it will wear away at the rate of only one inch every 10,000 years.

★ The carving of the four presidents in Mount Rushmore took more than fourteen years, but more than half of that time was spent waiting for more money. The final monument cost $989,992.32. More than two million people from all over the world visit it every year.

★ In 1937 Congress passed a bill saying that Susan B. Anthony should be carved beside the presidents, but they provided money only for the four heads that had been planned. There is, in any case, no room on the mountain for another head.

★ Gutzon Borglum died in 1941 before the final work on Mount Rushmore was completed. His son, Lincoln Borglum, finished his work as we see it today.